The Printforce Book Of
CHALLENGES

By David Saint

Illustrated throughout by Patrick Rose
with cover design by Jim Shorter
and art direction by
Ron Branagan

First edition 1988

First impression 1988

Saint, David, 1952-
   The Printforce book of challenges.
   1. Activities for young persons
   I. Title
   790.1'42

ISBN 0-948834-90-0

CONTENTS

INTRODUCTION

Young people thrive on challenge. Indeed, we all do.
Challenges form an important part of the programme of
all youth organisations, and also provide the basis for a
lot of the games that young people play.

The Printforce Book of Challenges brings together a
large number of activities that are translated into
Challenges. These activities have been loosely split into
categories for convenience of reference, and many of
them are suitable for use as personal challenges, one-to-
one challenges, team challenges, or challenges between
larger groups. They can be used by individuals in their
own time, by leaders as emergency 'fillers' in a meeting
that needs a little 'extra', or as part of a structured
programme.

We have included a chapter of Silly Challenges for light
relief, and one on Fund Raising through Challenges -
some ideas which are quite simple and practical, but
which may not be immediately obvious.

Finally, there is the Printforce Challenge. This is a
truly challenging competition open to readers of all
ages. A prize of £100.00 will be awarded to the first
reader to send in the correct answer. The next five
readers to send in correct answers will receive 10
Printforce Books of their choice. All other readers who
send in the correct answer will receive discount
vouchers for substantial savings on a future purchase of
Printforce Books.

Challenges are fun, exciting.... and good for us. Enjoy
the Challenges in this book, develop some of your own,
and have a go at our own Challenge - go on - we dare
you!

WHY CHALLENGES?

Life itself is a challenge. Throughout our existence we have to strive to survive. We have to compete with the elements; we have to compete with our fellows. Sometimes this leads to winners and losers; sometimes it simply leads to higher standards.

Winners and Losers

Let us address this question of winners and losers for a moment, as it has become a matter for some debate in recent years. As Challenges often involve competition, we should perhaps consider whether Competition is a Good Thing or a Bad Thing.

Some would argue that competition points up inequalities in people in areas over which they have little or no control - physical build, inherent intellect, upbringing, resources etc. They would argue that by making people feel they are losers, even in one or two areas only, we may lead them to view themselves as complete failures, and to lose self-respect. Winners, on the other hand, may become arrogant and over-bearing, and may come to believe that they have some sort of divine right always to be at the top of the tree.

Others would argue that competition encourages everybody to try that bit harder, thus raising standards overall. Perhaps this principle can be seen most keenly in sport, and in the business world. The teams or firms that want to succeed try harder, as do their competitors, ever pushing sporting achievements, or the provision of services or products, to new peaks of excellence.

As is so often the case, there is merit in both arguments. Perhaps we can draw from both of them to structure an approach to Challenges that enables each

OLYMPUS

individual young person to strive for excellence, and yet to feel a real sense of achievement when he or she reaches the upper level of their ability - which is almost certainly higher than that which they expected.

Personal Development

The principle of a Challenge is that there should be a target to strive for. To be worthwhile the target should be challenging, but it should also be achievable. If it were quite impossible, it would cease to be challenging, and become simply demoralising.

We can use Challenges to help ourselves develop. We often need to give ourselves good reasons for doing things we dislike or find difficult, but which we know we ought to do. By challenging ourselves, and turning the task into a contest or game, we make the unattractive activity that much more attractive. it is no longer a question of 'do I really have to do this?', but rather one of 'I wonder how quickly/thoroughly I can do this?'

The same will apply to young people. If asked to do something they do not like they will tend to rebel against it, but a challenge is hard to turn down, especially for a young person. 'Please peel 30 potatoes for us for lunch' is a most unattractive request. 'See how many potatoes you can peel in 13 minutes' is quite another matter - as long as the technique is not abused!

However, challenges need not only be applied to unpleasant activities. They can, as this book demonstrates, be great fun. They can help to develop abilities in the things we <u>want</u> to be able to do.

The best fuel for human activity is motivation. Without sufficient reason and desire to do something we will not do it - and this starts from the moment we wonder

whether to get out of bed in the morning! The element
of challenge, whether self-imposed or introduced from
outside, can often add the extra stimulus required for
action - and supreme action at that!

Take Care

As the nature of challenges is to push us to do more
than we might otherwise have intended, it is possible
that we could expose ourselves, or those in our care, to
some degree of danger, depending on the type of
challenge. We therefore have a responsibility to
ourselves and to others to think through the health and
safety implications of what we propose to do. Might
the challenged person be tempted to over-exert to a
dangerous extent? To get into dangerous situations? To
become so intent on achieving the goal as to become
unaware of (or unconcerned by) external safety factors?
Challenges need to stretch ourselves to our limits - not
beyond. If in any doubt, seek appropriate expert or
medical advice. Also ensure that you have all necessary
permissions and authority from owners of land or
property which may be affected by the activity.

Some challenges are trivial and just for fun; others are
more serious matters. For the latter, remember to
allow sufficient time for appropriate training or research
to increase their value. Challenges are about
development, not simply measuring where you are now.
With this in mind, it is often worth measuring what is
possible before the challenge, working up to the
challenge, and then measuring how far you have
progressed in the process.

Challenges for Everybody

Personal Challenge   In which you challenge yourself to
carry out an activity, or increase your ability in a
particular field.   The nature of the challenge, and

whether or not you carry it out, is a matter between yourself, your ambitions and your conscience. However, many people find this a useful mechanism to spur themselves on to greater things.

Individual Challenge In which one person in authority challenges another to do something, as a technique for encouraging that person to achieve something which might otherwise elude them. This might take the form of a youth leader challenging a member to work for a particular achievement, to give that person an extra spur to help them keep up with their peers, or to assume the level of responsibility appropriate to their age and position. A parent might use the technique as an alternative to threats and cajoling to obtain the required level of co-operation from their child. Rewards may or may not be associated with these challenges. Sometimes the achievement is reward enough.

One-to-one Challenge In which one person challenges another to a particular feat or activity. Clearly this is at its best when the rivals are reasonably evenly matched in their abilities, even if one has the advantage of brain, the other brawn. In the setting of a youth organisation, the leader may encourage such challenges to take place, and may or may not suggest the actual nature, or general subject matter of the challenge.

Team Challenge It is likely that this activity will be suggested by the leader. In planning the activity it is important to consider whether the teams are reasonably matched in their abilities, and to ensure that the activity is structured in such a way that all members of the team have some worthwhile part to play. This presents a good opportunity for team leaders to demonstrate and/or develop leadership skills.

Challenges for Large Groups Many individual units of youth organisations become somewhat insular in their activities, and if they do meet with members of other units it is often only for the annual swimming gala, or local football league. Great value and interest can be obtained from challenging another unit of your own youth organisation, or another one, to a different sort of activity. It may be best to discuss the proposal at leader level first, but then to allow the Challenge to be issued from the members of one unit to the members of another. It is important to ensure that acrimony does not creep in to the contest, and that the activity is carried out in a spirit of friendly rivalry.

CREATING CHALLENGES

Almost any activity can be turned into a Challenge, and for almost any number, or age group, of people.

The following tips may help you to develop Challenges of your own.

Try to quantify the Challenge. Express it in terms of How many.....How long....How high....How fast....How often....How cheaply....How well, etc.

Try to set clear targets or goals so that participants know what to try to achieve. Build in methods of measuring - during the Challenge as well as at the end of it if possible.

Try to leave no room for doubt. Make sure that the Challenge and its objective are unambiguous, and clearly understood by all concerned. make sure that the final results (and the starting point, if appropriate) are clearly recorded.

Be clear in your own mind about the purpose of having a Challenge. Is it to develop specific abilities in one or more of the participants (for example the main objective may be to develop leadership skills or a sense of responsibility in the team leader. Benefits to other members of the team may, in this case, simply be by-products). A clear understanding about why you are arranging the Challenge will help you to structure it so that your objectives are attained.

Make sure that adequate provision is made for safety arrangements, and that everybody knows what they are.

Make sure that, if any sort of reward or other incentive is planned, all participants know what it is, and in what circumstances they will qualify for it.

Look around you for inspiration for activities that might become Challenges. One often-used resource is the Guiness Book of Records, which contains countless activities of all descriptions which, by their very nature, are challenges anyway! Be warned - the level of achievement to beat feats which are contained in the Book is very high indeed. Still, it might be interesting to see just how near you can get to the World Record!

There are many other sources for ideas, however, if you mix a little imagination with your observations. You may read a story in the local paper about an unusual activity or feat which somebody else has attempted, and which you could also try - either in isolation or in direct competition with the person you read about. A piece in your own magazine or newsletter may spark off a thought.

Members' other interests may form the foundation of a Challenge. One person may have a particular interest or skill which they could challenge their peers to become proficient in. Other members could come up with counter-challenges based on their hobbies.

It might be a good idea to have a 'Challenges' slot as a regular part of your Programme, in which teams take it in turns to issue a Challenge to other teams. This has enormous potential for development, as each team strives to come up with more and more outrageous challenges and, of course, develops its own ability in the activity before issuing the Challenge, one presumes.

We would love to hear about some of the Challenges they come up with. You will write and tell us, won't you!

PHYSICAL ACTIVITY CHALLENGES

Perhaps the simplest and most common type of challenge is one concerning an individual's physical ability. The suggestions in this chapter are along these lines, and will therefore be quite familiar to you.

The difference to the young people challenged, however, is that the activities are presented in the form of a challenge, and not simply for the sake of the activity itself. Success and achievement become important in their own right. The emphasis turns from competition against one's fellows to competition with oneself. Where competition between people does occur it can be structured not simply to see who wins or does best, but how well each participant can do. Winners are not the only ones to receive praise and recognition - anybody who strives hard and achieves over and above what might have been expected is also a hero.

For many of the Challenges that follow, some form of written record chart will be a great help. The chart will show the development of individual ability within a particular time frame, or individual or team scores, depending on the activity. It is helpful if the fullest possible records can be kept to indicate improvements in achievement in the course of the Challenge as well as at the end of it. if a team effort is concerned, a method of recording individuals' contributions to the success of the whole is also very valuable. Motivation, which is what Challenges are all about, feeds on information and feedback.

Many of the activities in this chapter depend upon the participants exerting themselves more than might be usual for them. It is therefore particularly important to consider safety aspects in this respect. The average healthy child is unlikely to come to any harm from strenuous exercise - indeed it will be beneficial.

1 TON
CIRCUS
WORLDS
STRONGEST
KID

However, if the child is asthmatic, seriously overweight, or has some other relevant medical condition, advice should be sought before substantial physical effort is encouraged.

The following challenges can be adapted to suit individuals or groups, the equipment and locations available to them, and the level of ability or fitness of the participants. Each is intended as a 'prompt' to give you the basis for a Challenge of your own.

1.	How many layers of people can you use to build a human pyramid? Hints: Practice in sections, then make your final attempt as quickly as possible so that the lower layers do not tire too soon. Grade the participants carefully so that the heaviest and strongest are in the bottom layer. Have a camera ready to record the result!

2.	How many consecutive catches can be achieved by the players standing in a circle, with the 'thrower' in the centre. Try varying the diameter of the circle. Try the exercise again, catching with one hand only.

3.	How fast can two people cover a given distance tied together as for a three-legged race? How long would three people take tied together for a four-legged race? Five people? Six? Seven? How many people can you tie up like this, and still be able to make reasonable progress?

4.	Set up an obstacle course. How quickly can teams or individuals complete the course. How quickly can two people complete the course 'handcuffed' together? If it is safe to attempt it, see how quickly they can complete the course blindfolded.

5.   How far can participants throw a line? Try them out along the flat first, then test for height (as if throwing a grappling iron over a wall). How far can they throw a lifebelt? How accurately?

6.   How many lengths of the baths can the whole team swim in a given period of time? Everybody who can swim must contribute to the total.

7.   How long can an individual stand on one foot? Does it make any difference if they are blindfold?

8.   Produce a list of five <u>unusual</u> sports or sporting activities, having lined up a competent instructor in each. Challenge each member to select an activity they have not tried before, and to see how proficient they can become in it in (say) a six week period.

9.   Each team to challenge another in a sporting activity of their choice. The challenged team should be allowed an appropriate period to prepare or train for the contest.

10.   How far up a given tree or rope can members climb?

11.   How many consecutive skips can members achieve?

12.   Put together a 'basket' of activities. Challenge teams to compete against each other to find which team is best 'across the board'. The activities should be quite varied to suit a range of abilities including strength, stamina, accuracy, etc. A 'basket' might consist of press ups, sit ups, weight lifting, long jump, goal scoring, basket ball and balancing.

13.   With expert advice, set a target weight to be achieved by each member.   Some will need to build up their weight, and some will need to lose it.   Who can get nearest their optimum weight in a given period?

14.   Learn a new skill such as skateboarding, roller skating, ice skating, riding a horse or riding a bike.   Once the skill is mastered, set specific challenges relating to that activity.

15.   Select a target sport such as darts, archery or shooting.   Issue challenges for accuracy achieved. Within the safety constraints of the sport, set variations, such as increasing the distance, decreasing the size of the target etc.   If people get too good at hitting the bull, set a different part of the target as the desired objective to throw them off form!

16.   In the course of a season of a specific sport, keep a tally of achievements, such as goals scored, batting and bowling averages etc.   Ask each person challenged, to predict what 'score' they expect to achieve.   Encourage them to be ambitious!

17.   Challenge participants to test their endurance. Try long distance walking, jogging, road walking, cross-country running.   These activities do carry the risks of over-exertion, so do take sensible precautions such as ensuring that everybody is properly equipped (especially in terms of footwear) and that they know what to expect.   Have a qualified first-aider with the group, and arrange transportation form various points along the route for those who fall by the wayside.

18.   Challenge a rival team to a Wacky Race.   This

can take any one of a number of forms including Pram Pushes, Bath Pushes, Sedan Chair Races, Crazy Relay Races, etc. Merit is obtained not only for finishing first, but also for the craziest attitude to the activity!

19. Bring back the fads of ages past! Track down stilts, pogo sticks, space hoppers, etc., and build Challenges around them.

20. As a counterbalance to all the foregoing, challenge the members to see how little they can do for a given period. No movement, no sound, no exchanging glances - nothing!

PROBLEM SOLVING

The ability to solve problems of all   sorts is invaluable in our increasingly complex lives.   It is also an ability which is perhaps diminished by the ever greater availability of labour-saving devices, and help and support available to us.

Problem solving can be broken down into a number of stages which makes the process much more manageable. The first step is to identify and define the problem, and the elements of it.   The next step is to identify what needs to happen for the problem not to be there - what needs to be changed.   Finally, we have to identify the action necessary to bring about this change.   Depending on the nature of the problem this may require the marshalling of specific human or material resources.   It can frequently require some lateral thinking.   The cleansing of the Augean Stables is a good example of this!

These steps, in various forms, can be applied to most of the following Challenges.   Participants can work in teams or individually as seems appropriate.

1.   Supply each team or individual with a thoroughly tangled length of string, rope, chain or wire. Challenge them to untangle it in the shortest possible time.   As it may be difficult to ensure that each team gets an equally tangled length, an alternative strategy would be to challenge each team to tangle the material to their satisfaction in a given period, and then pass it to the next team for untangling.   It is surprisingly difficult to thoroughly tangle something when you <u>do</u> want to!

2.   Compile a crossword linked to your training scheme, or to a particular subject of relevance to your group.   Challenge each team to solve it.

THUD!
THUD!

This is another opportunity to get each team to do your work for you. Provide them with a crossword grid and ask them to set the answers and clues. A duplicate copy of the blank grid is then passed to another team for solving. Challenge teams or individuals to work their way through progressively more difficult crosswords from simple 'picture clue' crosswords to the Times Crossword. Invite a crossword enthusiast to explain the techniques of cryptic clues first. You might be surprised at the results!

3.   Now get out of that! Define or create a situation which individuals or teams have to cope with. Clearly it will be more fun and more challenging to put them physically in the situation, but this may not always be possible. For example, they might be 'stranded on a desert island' with a few specific items of equipment with which to feed themselves, signal, and try to escape. Perhaps their key equipment has to be 'rescued from a vehicle trapped in a quagmire'. Small teams are probably best for these exercises.

4.   The Great Egg Race. Another Challenge inspired by a television programme. Each team is supplies with an assortment of equipment, and a problem to be solved. For example, they might be required to develop a wind turbine, an alarm clock, or a go-kart. The complexity of the project will naturally depend on the age group of the participants. A few pieces of equipment which have no relevance to the project whatever (as far as you know!) should be supplied to confuse the issue slightly!

5.   Murder Mystery. Set up the scene of a crime. Murder is usually particularly popular. A number of clues and less helpful pieces of evidence can

be left for the budding detectives to examine, and from which they have to deduce what happened, and who did it.   Spice might be added by supplying some 'witnesses' for questioning. However, for this to be successful they will have had to be very well rehearsed, and will need to have stories that fit the 'facts' which you have decided upon.   Indoors, clues might include finger prints on very dusty tabletops,   half smoked cigarettes, a forgotten glass etc.   Outdoors, the detectives might find footprints, tyre tracks, etc.

6.   Develop some codes to be cracked as a Challenge. Better still, incorporate them into another Challenge.   Books on codes are readily available, although they should be reasonably simple for this exercise so you should be able to develop your own.   Perhaps each team would care to develop a code of its own which it will use for communication between members.   Members of other teams will need to try to crack their opponents' codes in the course of the exercise which may only involve the use of codes as an incidental part of it.

7.   Persuading other people to accept your point of view is often a very serious problem.   Hold a debate, in which a reasonable number of members have an opportunity to state their point of view. Hold a poll on the subject before and after the debate to see how far opinion has shifted.   A method of developing these skills to a quite high degree is to ask debaters to exchange roles - with little warning.   The key protagonists are asked to state their positions on the issue in question. They are then challenged to reverse roles, and argue the case they imagine their opponent would put.   The objective is to win the argument, not to get across the point of view they started with,

so there is no advantage in putting the opponent's case weakly! Topics may be close to home, such as a discipline issue within the organisation, or whether to take action on a local environment issue. Alternatively they may be national or international issues such as nuclear disarmament, Third World debt, etc.

8.   How many people can stand on a single house brick at once? Try other variations such as trying to get as many people as possible into a car (but not whilst it is being driven!) or into a telephone box. Any serious attempt at this exercise requires a great deal of planning, and probably a number of practice runs. Develop a few new variations of your own. How many people can sit in an arm chair simultaneously, for example?

9.   Identify a problem you have walked away from, and force yourself to go back and try and solve it. This is most successful as a form of self-discipline, but you can also challenge others to do the same, either in respect of any problem they may choose, or a specific one you have identified. the problem might be practical, such as finding a way to repair something that is broken. It might be personal, concerned with a difficult relationship which needs to be sorted out. By turning the problem into a challenge you improve your attitude to it, and thus your emotional ability to tackle it.

10. Have you ever been mildly curious about why something is the way it is, but have never really bothered to find out the answer? Challenge the members to find it out for you! Why are house bricks usually red? Why does the television picture disappear into a point of light when the

TOP STAR
SPORT

set is turned off? The question may require them
to think through the answer logically. They may
have to do a degree of research to find the
answer.

11.   Identify a problem that faces your organisation.
       Lack of funds?   Lack of leaders or helpers?
       Lack of members?   Boring, repetitive
       programmes?   Challenge groups of members to
       'brainstorm' the problem and to come up with
       some solutions.   Encourage them not to dismiss
       the seemingly ridiculous - such suggestions can
       often be developed into practical solutions.

12.   This Challenge can either provide you with an
       opportunity to solve a problem of your own, or
       you can 'engineer' a problem to be solved. Supply
       the members with something which needs to be
       repaired.   Depending on their ages and abilities
       this might be a kite in pieces, a clock or radio
       that does not function, or a car that will not
       start.   It would probably be fairest if you were
       reasonably confident that the fault can be
       corrected, and that any necessary spare parts are
       available! You could choose to confuse the issue,
       however, by having too many assorted spare parts
       available!

13.   Supply an extract from a piece of text, and
       challenge the members to identify its source. It
       might be part of the instructions for a game such
       as monopoly or snakes and ladders. It might be
       an operating manual for a washing machine or
       word processor.   Each team could be supplied
       with five or six to solve - it will add to the
       confusion if some are quite similar to others.
       Extra marks for extra accuracy, of course.
       Naming the make or even the model would be
       good going. Quoting the serial number would be

downright suspicious!

14.   Set a problem that needs to be solved with some
       form of construction.   Supply the necessary
       materials, and state any restrictions that you may
       wish to impose.   Once again, it can help to
       hinder the teams by supplying a number of pieces
       of equipment that are not relevant - as far as
       you know!   The problem might be to work out a
       way of lifting a heavy weight, or crossing a
       crocodile-infested river, or sounding an alarm at
       sunrise without the benefit of an alarm clock.

15.   To prove that necessity is the mother of
       invention, carry out a similar exercise to the one
       above,   but supply one too few items of
       equipment.   Teams might be required to erect a
       tent without tentpegs, cook sausages without a
       frying pan or, that old favourite, light a fire
       without matches!

16.   What would you do if......?   Invent an emergency
       situation, and give teams or individuals a specific
       amount of time to deal with it, in relation to the
       amount of time they would have if the occurrence
       was real.   You might actually stage the situation,
       or simply describe it.   If you plan to stage it in
       public,   make sure that the real emergency
       services know what you are planning in case they
       are called out by a member of the public!   They
       will be less than amused!   Teams might be asked
       to describe how they would deal with the
       situation if they saw somebody lying at the edge
       of the road, or if they found a car with the keys
       in the ignition, unattended.   Perhaps they will
       spot smoke coming from a first floor window, or
       will find a boy with his head caught in fence
       railings.   Once the teams have reacted, or
       described their reactions, discuss these to see

which was the most effective, and what each could learn from the others.

17. Many children are becoming very keen on computer adventure games (as opposed to the 'Space Invader' type) in which they have to pit their wits against the computer to achieve some objective. There are a number of ways this can provide programme material. Perhaps you will issue a simple challenge based on individuals' ability to progress deep into the game. Perhaps you will challenge members to develop their own simple computer game - some of them will have quite sophisticated skills! Alternatively, you may use the principle - questions which, when answered correctly, lead on to another question - to devise a game of your own for which a computer is not required.

18. Given adequate interest and ability, challenge individuals or small teams to solve problems in games such as chess or bridge. Such 'set piece' problems are often published in newspapers or magazines. Alternatively you may create your own, or invite each team to invent one with which to challenge another team.

19. Obtain sufficient identical cheap puzzle books. Supply one to each team and challenge them to solve as many puzzles as they can in a given time.

20. Make your own jigsaw. You might choose a national flag, or a page of a book familiar to the members, or a page of a newspaper. Either challenge each team to reassemble the cut up item in the fastest possible time, or produce identical sets for each team to put together simultaneously.

MONSTERS & DUNGEONS
7

CREATIVITY

A blank piece of paper, or an unmoulded mass of clay, presents a challenge to any creative person. Creativity is the process of responding to the challenge of raw materials or opportunity, to turn them into something useful, something desirable. The following suggestions are some ideas for presenting creative opportunities as challenges. You will doubtless be able to develop others yourself.

1. Challenge individuals to disguise themselves so that they are not recognised. This may be tested in a number of ways. Participants may line up before judges who have to try to identify them. A more interesting method would be to challenge the participants to mingle at an event and not be identified by the judges who would also be there. They should be required to gather a range of information at the event to ensure that they are there for some time. You might supply a range of disguises including old clothes, wigs, hats, false beards etc., or you might leave this entirely to the participants' ingenuity.

2. Soapbox Corner. Challenge members to stand on the soapbox to berate their peers about a topic close to their hearts. Each person should be allowed three minutes to put across a case and, in the best tradition of Speaker's Corner, constructive heckling should be allowed. Some practice may be called for, especially in dealing with shouted comments from the floor, and care should be taken that the whole exercise is carried out with good humour.

3. Challenge members to demonstrate their skills with the written word. They may be challenged to write a poem, perhaps on a given subject, and

read it to the others members. Perhaps they will
be challenged to write a letter - not just to a
friend but to a local councillor or Member of
Parliament, about an issue that concerns them.
They may be challenged to an editorial feat that
requires some staying power, such as a logbook,
diary, or regular newsletter. In these cases, make
sure that the sense of challenge is maintained,
and that momentum is not lost.

4.   It is a great challenge to try to get something
      published. It is very difficult, and those who
      make the attempt should be ready for much
      disappointment.

      However, there are a number of opportunities, and
      given a general challenge to get something
      published somewhere, some members may be
      successful. Opportunities include articles in the
      Church or Parish magazine, your own Newsletter
      (although you may exclude this as being too
      easy!), the local paper (either a small article or a
      Letter to the Editor), or a regional or national
      paper. There are other opportunities including
      special interest magazines and papers, publications
      serving your own organisation, and children's
      comics. Many publications have a special section
      for contributions such as jokes, news and letters
      from children. The really ambitious might try to
      get a book published .... you will remember to
      offer Printforce the opportunity to publish it,
      won't you!

5.   Try a new art form - pottery, sculpture, serious
      photography, macrame, etc. Obtain the services
      of a talented volunteer to demonstrate the craft
      and help the members develop the techniques,
      before they attempt the final challenge of putting
      their skills into practice and making a New

Creation with their new skill!

6.   Challenge members to take a photograph of an everyday object from an unusual angle. This requires quite a bit of creativity in looking at things in a different way, as the photograph must be very confusing to look at, and yet instantly recognisable when you know what it is! A camera with a lense that enables you to take close-up shots would be a great advantage.

7.   Challenge members to get a pen pal from as far away as possible. Some may already have contacts in other countries, otherwise they will have to use their ingenuity to find ways of making contact. The challenge might include a requirement to find out as much about the pen pals, their way of life, etc. There may also be a challenge to correspond in a foreign language, or to maintain the correspondence over a minimum period or number of letters exchanged.

8.   Challenge the members to write and tell a story - not to their peers this time, but to a group of children in a younger age group. This might be an individual effort, or the results of a small team working together. The team might also co-operate in the reading, making it more interesting to listen to.

9.   Challenge the members to a sandcastle competition. You do not need to be by the seaside for this as a sack or two of sandpit sand from a builder's merchant would not be very expensive. You do not need to be under 10 to enjoy the exercise either!

10.   Set up height and time trials for home made kites, or hot air balloons, or gliders. Challenge

members to design and build their own, and to compete against each other for the most effective construction.

11.   Supply a number of packs of playing cards and challenge teams to build the largest and most elaborate house of cards that they can. Very still conditions will naturally be required, and cheating should be firmly discouraged or you will get nowhere!   New cards are more effective; old cards may be more readily available!

12.   Supply a number of unusual shapes or objects and challenge members to construct pictures using those items as the foundation.   Alternatively, mark a number of lines on a piece of paper, a photocopy of which is given to each team. They are required either to make any picture they wish from the lines, or to try to recreate what you had in mind when you drew them! In any event, you should have some idea of what you expect them to do, to make sure that the exercise is not impossible!

13.   Give each team a list of, say, five words. Each team is challenged to make up a short story containing all the words. A typical list might include a spare tyre, contradictory, elephant, hitch-hiker and sparkle.

14.   Supply the first line of a limerick, and challenge members to write the rest of the verse. To make this truly challenging, select a particularly difficult word for which they have to find a rhyme - this should lead to some excruciating last lines!

15.   Challenge teams to record a song. Unless they are extremely good they will not get a record

made, but they should be able to put together a tape recording of their performance. They may or may not be required to write the words and/or music, and to provide their own orchestral accompaniment. You may care to provide reasonably favourable recording conditions for each team in turn if you can find a room with good acoustics, and obtain the use of a good tape recorder - with stereo microphones if possible.

16. Whether or not as a prelude to the above Challenge, members could be challenged to take up and develop an ability in a musical instrument. Depending on your resources and the abilities of the members you might provide mass tuition in something 'simple' like a penny whistle, or each member might choose their own instrument to learn. If it is possible to bring them all together for a mass performance as an incentive to developing reasonable ability in a reasonable length of time, so much the better.

17. Invent a children's toy or game. Construct it, and field test it on a small group of children of a suitable age. It is extremely important that a great deal of attention is paid to the safety of the toy, so that it is appropriate to the age group. Small pieces, sharp pieces and painted pieces can all present hazards, especially to younger children.

18. Although many schools now teach carpentry to girls and cookery to boys there is still room for youth organisations to help each sex develop a degree of independence in activities in which they indulge less frequently. Select a challenge for your members, therefore, which requires them to master and demonstrate a skill more frequently or traditionally demonstrated by the opposite sex.

Boys will benefit from being able to iron, or wash socks, or make a pavlova.   Girls will find it useful to be able to make a small table, change the oil in a car, or put up a shelf.

19.   Whether or not you supply the wherewithal, challenge individuals to grow a plant from seed. You might go for quantity, with a traditional sunflower growing contest, or you may go for quality, with an attempt to grow something quite difficult.

20.   Provide members with a pebble or stone and some poster paints, and challenge them to turn it into a work of art.   They might use the smooth surface of a pebble as a 'canvas' on which to paint, or they may find that the irregular shape of the stone suggests a particular object.   In this case they will paint the stone to emphasise this resemblance.   Such an exercise is a great creative challenge, as it requires an ability to see the stone not for what it is, but for what it might be.   Finished results can be greatly enhanced, and their survival made more certain, by the application of two or more coats of clear varnish, once the original paint has dried.

CHALLENGES THROUGH GAMES

Games are for fun, and every programme of activities should include some games for sheer enjoyment, and letting off steam. As with the other forms of activity we have explored, by turning a game into a challenge we add an edge to the activity, giving it greater interest and appeal. The following suggestions are largely adaptions of existing games which lend themselves to this sort of treatment. You can doubtless think of many more yourself.

1. Select a game which is normally for two players, and play on your own against yourself. This is a very interesting way of developing techniques in the game, but it requires a great deal of self-discipline to play each 'hand' as if you had no knowledge of the other.

2. Hold a Scrabble Championship. This might be to find the person who can achieve the highest score, or you might run three or four games at once, the object being for each group of players to achieve the highest possible corporate score, whilst adhering to all the normal rules of the game.

3. Trivial Pursuit has become immensely popular, and has spawned numerous spin-offs. The principle can easily be adapted to subject matter relevant to your organisation. Sets of questions and answers should be prepared in, say, 6 categories, and teams or individuals are challenged to answer them if they can. It is not essential to use the board game format of the original, but this does add an extra dimension which lifts the activity beyond being a simple quiz.

4. Challenge the members to participate in a

Scavenger Hunt. Remember that this is to be a Challenge, so the items to be collected will be obscure in the extreme, making allowance for the age of the participants, of course. Items to be obtained might include a German Sausage, the pen of the Leader's Aunt, a Greek dictionary, a snowball, etc.

5. Take a television or radio panel game or contest and adapt it to suit your own circumstances for a Challenge. There are many to choose from, including Just a Minute, What's my Line, It's a Knockout etc. You can either add additional humour and enjoyment by adhering as closely as possible to the original format (even having your own guest 'celebrities'!), or adapt the idea so dramatically that it becomes almost unrecognisable.

6. Challenge the youngsters (and any oldsters who would benefit from it!) to go for a week without watching television, finding other ways of amusing themselves. They should keep a log showing any lapses they had (and why) but more importantly, what activities they found to do instead. You might add a further challenge, in the form of a contest to see who can come up with the most unusual, original or ridiculous alternative activity.

7. Hold a Hopscotch Championship, particularly if the members are somewhat 'past it'. Such children's games may sound silly, but can be quite challenging to lumbering fifteen-year olds!

8. Given suitable facilities, and perhaps a bit of tuition, stage a Golf or Putting Challenge. If the members are reasonably mature, and prepared to take the activity seriously you might find a private or municipal course willing to give them

HOME
SWEET
HOME
WAHHH!
TV TIMES

an exclusive session at some off peak time. Failing this, set up a Crazy Golf course, and challenge the members to make their way around that.

9.   Have you ever thought of staging a Crazy Blow Football Match? I thought not!

9.   Back to outdoor sports, you could consider introducing the members to Croquet, or Boules (French Bowls). It can be quite a challenge to learn how to play the game if it is new to you, and then there is plenty of challenge in trying to beat the opposition.

10.   Challenge the members to set up and play a game of life-size chess, or snakes and ladders, or draughts. The members are the 'pieces' which move about the board. How they create the board, snakes and ladders, dice etc., is up to them. This calls for some creative thinking, and then provides a lot of laughs as the game is played - as long as the action is fast.

11.   Certain board games can go on - and on. Play a marathon game of Monopoly, or Go or some such. Alternatively, have a Games Evening, to which members are encouraged to bring their favourite games - clearly marked with their names. See how many difference games each person can complete in a given time. This can lead to some hectic activity - especially if the rules of some games are new to some people.

12.   For a real Challenge, invite the members to learn Bridge. This is unlikely to appeal to many people below sixteen, and many above that age may find it tiresome to start with. It is important to ask an enthusiastic and articulate player to introduce

the game to them, and for it to be kept simple at first. Allow a sufficient period to elapse for some basic skills to be acquired, and then hold a simple Bridge drive. be warned, some people will loose interest quickly. Others may become hooked!

13.   Whatever the age range of your members, invite them to devise a game to be played by children younger than them. This should be quite practical as they should still be able to remember what they enjoyed, and were able to do at that age. It may be that they will need a little guidance to help them get started - perhaps some basic parameters such as 'it must be a board game', or 'it must involve a ball'. Thereafter, the members should devise the game, invent the rules, produce any necessary equipment, try the game out themselves and modify it as necessary - before field testing it on a group of children in the target age group that you had previously lined up for this purpose, unknown to your own members!

15.   New Games are a fast growing genre of activities that are based on the principle of competing against an outside force, or yardstick, rather than competing against each other. It might be an activity in which all the members have to help each other defeat the pull of gravity, or it might be an attempt to better another group's record for an activity. Select a New Game, and use this as a different form of Challenge in which the members are not trying to beat their colleagues, but are trying to achieve a <u>corporate</u> feat.

16.   Devise a game of Crazy Snap, Crazy Pelmanism, or some other simple card game. It becomes crazy because you substitute real objects for cards. This will require some thinking through,

but should provide a lot of laughs.   The biggest challenge may be in devising the game!   Perhaps the members should be involved in this as well.

17.   Kim's Game is popular with many organisations, and there are many variations on it.   Essentially, members are required to remember the positions, and or names, of a number of objects, and then recall them later.   The activity can be made more challenging by using highly unusual objects that they would have difficulty in identifying, or very similar objects which it is hard to tell apart. (You might show a tray of nine apples arranged in a square, for example, and then, after having given the members time to study the tray and recovered it, asking them to state which apple had no stalk).

18.   Many people are not content with playing games properly these days, and there is a great deal of 'trick' snooker, soccer etc., going on, in which players carry out 'set piece' shots which are very dramatic.   You could either challenge the members to stage a 'set piece' you define, in the chosen sport, or challenge them to invent one of their own.

19.   Back to the playground now.   Challenge the members to stage conker fights, tiddlywink tournaments, or other pursuits of those halceon days.

20.   Set up a fairground day, in which a range of fairground activities is replicated, and challenge the members to do their best at each activity - for no charge of course!   This can be done very inexpensively, and is a good opportunity for parents, or older children, to help out.   Games could include Tin Can Alley, coconut shy, ping-

pong balls into jars, kicking footballs into buckets, crockery smashing, and throwing darts at playing cards. You can doubtless think of many others. If it all goes well you might stage the event again, but this time open the doors to the public, charge, and raise some funds!

KNOWLEDGE

Challenges about knowledge can be based on how much
the participants know, how much they can manage to
learn, or how much they can deduce about a matter
from information supplied. The first of these is perhaps
the most common, taking the form of quizzes and such
like; the second and thirds are perhaps the more
valuable, as they involve a degree of mental exercise
and personal extension, beyond mere recall.   The
Challenges in this section range across these categories,
but many of them can be adapted to fit into a different
category, or, indeed, to contain elements of each.

1. Challenge members to learn a valuable new skill
    such as Life Saving or First Aid.   Do not leave
    this as an open-ended Challenge with no climax
    (other than the gaining of an Award, perhaps).
    Link the training to a specific outcome, such as a
    promised boating activity, hill walking expedition
    etc., for which such skills may prove essential.
    Thereafter, hold regular 'snap' exercises to keep
    the members on their toes - a sort of perpetual
    Challenge.   If a skill such as life saving is not
    used from time to time it becomes less
    instinctive, and less valuable.   Fortunately, real
    life occasions for its use are encountered by most
    of us somewhat infrequently, so exercises are
    necessary to keep the skill fresh.

2. If some members are slow or reluctant to move
    forward in your organisation's award scheme or
    training programme, use Challenges as a trigger
    for action.   You may secretly challenge an
    individual to complete a particular requirement
    before a set time, such as his or her birthday, or
    the end of the month or term.   You may
    challenge the whole group publicly to achieve as
    much as possible between them by a given time

perhaps engendering a situation in which they help each other, competing against <u>you,</u> to show you that they jolly well <u>can</u> do it, and are not as hopeless as you suggest!

3.   Challenge the members to learn specific phrases in a foreign language. Options for you to consider might include one language, or a range of languages; phrases you select, or phrases selected by the members; translations provided by you or researched by the members. Again, it would be worth linking the Challenge to a final purpose, such as a day-trip to France, a visit by somebody from another country, or an International Evening, in which the games, songs, activities and refreshments are reflective of a particular part of the world.

4.   Challenge the members to learn the knots necessary for a specific purpose. Again, you may or may not specify what they are, depending on the age and ability of the members; they may have to research them themselves. The purpose might be a simple pioneering project, an activity such as a boating expedition, or the construction of a training board of knots for younger members.

5.   Challenge each member to select a highly unusual subject in which to become an expert. Set a date by which this information is to be assimilated, and create some opportunity for the knowledge to be used or displayed. You might need to offer some suggestions, and perhaps be prepared to point the members in the general direction of experts, relevant organisations, or reference books. Subjects might range from campanology to chipmunks, palaeontology to postcards. This Challenge may result in a little extra knowledge for some - it may lead to a

life-long fascination for others!

6. Build a Challenge around leaf and tree recognition. Provide a chart with a number of leaf outlines on it, and challenge the members to collect a leaf to match as many of them as possible. Alternatively, provide a blank chart, and challenge them to fill it with as many different named varieties as possible. Provide each team with some coloured ribbon or wool, and challenge them to tie their colour round one example of each of, say, six named species of tree in a given area.

7. Depending on their age and experience, challenge each team to pitch a simple tent in a difficult way. They should have to pitch it against the clock, or completely in the dark, or without the practical assistance of the team leader.

8. Challenge the members, as a group, to learn to dance. You may choose ballroom, or Latin American, or ballet, or contemporary. Bring in an outside instructor for the purpose. As with all other such Challenges, you should arrange an opportunity to implement the skill at the end of the course, in this case in the form of a party, or dance, with or without 'outsiders' such as parents!

9. Challenge members to demonstrate the extent of their local knowledge. There are a number of ways to do this. State a location and a direction, and challenge them to describe what can be seen there as accurately as possible, from memory. State a starting point and destination and ask them to describe the best route from one to the other, in such a way as would be understood by a stranger to the area.

10.   Set up a route using only compass bearings, and challenge the members to complete it with pin point accuracy, including precisely following the stated number of paces.

11.   Set up a game of snakes and ladders, except the snakes and the ladders have the same effect as each other - if you land on one and answer a question correctly you ascend to the top. If you are incorrect, you slide down to the bottom!

12.   Play Just a Minute, but hand out the subjects a week in advance - all subjects to all players. They are to prepare themselves so that they can speak for just a minute on the subject, and so that they can sensibly challenge their peers if they deviate etc.   The subjects should be somewhat obscure, or ones in which you would like them to extend their knowledge!

13.   Play Call My Bluff.   This is similar in a way, except that it is concerned only with individual words.   Here are two suggestions for the game. In the first game you would supply one member of a team with a word which relates to your training programme, and he would talk about that word, either accurately describing it, or being deliberately incorrect.   For example, he may be given the name of a knot, which he would <u>almost</u> correctly describe how to tie, and would then describe incorrect uses for it.   The opposing team has to decide whether the description is true or false.   In the second game you would play it just as on television; the words chosen are all in the dictionary, but are so obscure nobody has heard of them!   The game is played as above.

14.   Stage a Safety Challenge.   Set up an unsafe situation (carefully!) such as a room with a

number of dangerous features. Challenge the members to take a thorough look at it, and describe the steps that would have to be taken to make it safe again.

15. Set up a research project and challenge the members to carry it out. Perhaps you will ask them to research the suitability of a particular location for a full day activity, or a Summer camp site. Perhaps they will research the feasibility of a summer playgroup scheme, which they might run if it turns out to be necessary and practical.

16. Just for fun, hold a Name That Tune contest. Prepare a tape recording of short pieces of music, and challenge the members to name as many of them as possible. They may be your organisation's favourite songs, hits from the charts, popular classics, hymn tunes...whatever you like.

17. Issue copies of specialist magazines to teams, and then ask them questions on the subject. You may leave the magazines with them so they can research the answers, or remove them, forcing them to learn and remember. Suitable subjects would include various sports, boating, model railways, aircraft, cooking, nature, etc.

18. Produce a number of Odd Objects, and challenge the members to work out what they are for. They may be obscure items you keep in the back of a drawer in the kitchen or toolshed, specialist tools you borrow from a local tradesman, or old fashioned items borrowed from a local museum.

19. Put together a montage of famous faces cut out of magazines, newspaper, etc., and challenge the

members to identify as many of them as possible.

20.   Challenge the members to compile 20 questions to confound you!   You may specify the subject matter, or give them an open field.   They must be able to provide the answers should you fail, and be able to verify them!

DISCIPLINE

This may seem strange subject matter for a book of
Challenges, and yet it is perhaps one of the most useful
uses of the extra incentive that Challenges bring. The
following Challenges are worded for use by the person
reading them, rather than for imposition on other
people. However, in some circumstances you may
choose to challenge other people to one or more of
them. It should be remembered that the response to a
Challenge comes from within, and in the case of
discipline this is even more the case. We can be
bullied, bribed or otherwise coerced to accept discipline,
but the hardest, most valuable and most effective is self
discipline - a personal decision to take a course of
action which may not be the obvious choice, but which
is obviously right. Discipline is good for you. Try it!

1.   Challenge yourself to give something up. It may
      be an indulgence, such as cigarettes or chocolate.
      It may be a habit, such as complaining, or
      boasting. You may well need additional
      mechanisms to help you succeed, such as setting
      short term goals first (one day without, one week
      without etc.). It may help to identify an
      alternative which can be used whenever you might
      otherwise have or do that which you are giving
      up. Keep a log of each day of success to
      encourage you, and each failure to prod your
      conscience. It can help to link this Challenge to
      an occasion such as New Year (Resolution), or
      Lent. It can also help if you tell those around
      you what you are trying to do, so that they do
      not put temptation your way, and stop you if you
      seem likely to lapse!

2.   Challenge yourself to do something you do not
      like. You will know what that is far better than
      I, but here are some ideas! Keep the ironing up

to date; keep the car clean; make a specific space to play with your children; fill in forms on time; make yourself go to something you do not expect to enjoy such as the Ballet, or a pop concert.

3.   Befriend somebody you (and others) tend to shun. This needs to be done sensibly and sensitively, and for the right reasons. However, there are many people in our communities who for some reason are unpopular, or just not popular (which is different). There is frequently no good reason for this, as you will discover as you get to know them. Lonely people are not always on their own. One of the worst forms of loneliness is being with a body of people, and yet not a part of them. Look around your Church, or club, or place of work, or street, and see who always gets left out.

4.   Challenge yourself to do something you are afraid of. Many of us have irrational fears, and one effective way of tackling them is deciding to face the fear, and see if it is really as bad as we think. Often fear of the (supposedly) unknown is the worst of all. Challenge yourself to travel in a lift, climb the church tower, pick up a spider, ride a bicycle, go to a dance....

5.   Challenge yourself not to break <u>any</u> rules in the course of a day. This should include all the 10 Commandments (do you know what they all are?!), the Highway Code (including the speed limit!), office rules, and the normal tenets of polite civilised society. Is it impossible, or does it make for a more pleasant life-style? A combination of the two, I would suspect.

6.   Challenge yourself to begin a regimen which you

have occasionally thought of starting, but never actually got round to. Make Today the Day! You might start a diet, take up a Bible reading course, keep a regular diary, or begin regular exercising, for example.

7.   Challenge yourself to become able to do something that you cannot do. Don't give up! Examples might include learning to drive a car, cook, hang wallpaper, play golf....what would you add to the list?

8.   As an extension of the above, challenge yourself to develop a greater degree of independence. Whatever your age or sex you will tend to rely on somebody for certain forms of help. Identify those areas in which you are perhaps unnecessarily dependent, and develop your ability in those areas so that, should the situation arise, you could cope.

9.   Challenge yourself to budget properly, and exercise control over expenditure. This would also be a good challenge to put to children with their pocket money. Establish the amount of income, note down all the essential and unavoidable expenditure, make an allowance for savings towards larger irregular bills and then decide what you wish to (and should do) with what (if anything!) is left. Keep a record of how actual expenditure worked out in relation to your budget, and this will help you plan more accurately for future budgets.

10.   Look through your Address Book, and identify a friend or relative who you have neglected for some time. Arrange to visit them, or write them a letter, or telephone them. It is so easy to lose touch with people that we do not come into contact with as a matter of course. That letter

or phone call could mean so much.

As we said at the beginning of this chapter, self-discipline is, by its nature, a very personal thing. You will know the areas of your life-style that would benefit from attention of this sort. It is a strange irony of the human psyche that we often avoid doing things because we think we will be less happy as a result; in practice they frequently make a positive contribution to our quality of life.

SILLY CHALLENGES

After all the effort of the rest of the book, and the serious nature of the last chapter, we thought it would be an idea to lighten the mood with a brief collection of really crazy ideas!

1. Challenge the members to sleep in the most unusual place they can think of. Check out their proposed place of repose first, to ensure that it is safe!

2. Challenge the members to arrive at a given location by means of the most unusual form of transport they can arrange. Again, safety factors should be considered.

3. Challenge the members to arrive at a given event in the most unusual attire they can lay their hands on. The well tried question 'are you wearing that for a bet?' becomes not far off the mark!

4. Challenge the members to eat something they have never eaten before. This may be something they select, or you might lay on a particularly exotic meal for them. Be sure that you are prepared to eat what you expect them to consume - you may have to!

5. Hold a gurning contest, in which you challenge the members to pull the most gruesome face they can.

6. You might have a wellie-throwing challenge. As this is now a little 'old hat' you might devise a variation on the theme, like old hat throwing for example.

7.   It crossed my mind to suggest you challenge the
        members to find a needle in a haystack. If you
        cannot find an understanding farmer to allow this,
        or if you feel the suggestion is not so much crazy
        as beyond belief, you might dream up a near
        alternative. Hunt the thimble in the dark, for
        example?

8.   Challenge the members to name, or produce, as
        many things as possible beginning with a certain
        letter, or of a certain colour. You may place
        restrictions, such as nobody must leave the
        premises, or each item must be small enough to
        fit into a pillowcase. It depends how crazy you
        feel, really!

9.   Challenge the members to produce the most
        highly decorated wellington boots they can devise.
        You might equip yourself with a number of pairs
        from a few jumble sales to avoid complaints from
        less artistically-minded parents!

10.   Challenge the members to devise a Challenge that
        they can do that you cannot.

EEEK!

FUND RAISING THROUGH CHALLENGES

Almost as an appendix to the main book, we thought it might be a good idea to address ourselves to the use of Challenges as a fund raising vehicle, as they do rather lend themselves to this purpose. The few examples in this chapter may give you all the ideas you need. You might take the principle, and apply it to other ideas you find in the book, or make up yourself.

1. Publicise the fact that you are challenging yourselves to clean as many cars, shine as many shoes, or whatever, as you can in a given period of time. Invite your supporters, or the public, to submit their cars, or shoes as appropriate for participation in this extravaganza. Naturally they will pay for the privilege of your attentions, so you must ensure that speed is not achieved at the expense of efficiency. You may also obtain sponsors on the basis of the number of jobs completed in the given period. The element of urgency, and striving against the clock, will add extra impact to your fund raising drive, and hopefully attract more support and custom than the activity might otherwise warrant.

2. You might also obtain additional support for a more usual form of sponsored activity if it is presented as a Challenge. Sponsored Walks and Swims are very commonplace, but to be sponsored to take part in a Swimming Challenge or Walk Against the Clock is a little different. One nice gimmick which is occasionally used is to try to walk the 'equivalent of the distance across Africa', or swim 'the equivalent of the Pacific', or climb 'the equivalent of Everest'. The achievements of each individual are added together, and if you have a large enough number of athletic enough people these feats are quite

achievable - and irresistible for the local press!

3.   A sponsored Jailbreak is quite a popular activity now. Participants are challenged to get as far away from a given point (preferably a real jail!) as they can in a given time. They are sponsored according to the distance they achieve. Frequently they are required to do this without money, and often they have to start off dressed in 'traditional' prison garb - complete with broad arrows all over it! There have been instances of people using their persuasive powers (and a little forward planning) to get as far as New York (from the UK). This is a little unusual, but distances in excess of 50 miles are not uncommon.

4.   Challenge a potential supporter to match the funding you are able to raise. For example, if you are trying to raise £15,000 for a new minibus, and you want to get the major local employer to contribute, do not write to ask for a donation. Instead, challenge him to offer to match the money that your members are able to raise by a certain date. he may wish to set a limit, which is fine. This sort of approach may appeal to him, may well appeal to the local press, and will also present a challenge to your members - to raise half the sum needed pretty quickly!

5.   At fetes and fairs people find it very difficult to resist a challenge - unless nobody challenges them. Make sure you have plenty of sideshows that give people the opportunity to show just how clever they really are, and have people on each stall to challenge the punters to show their worth. Sometimes the only reward they will need is self-satisfaction - prizes may not be necessary. Activities might include ringing the bell with a

smash of the sledgehammer, getting a hoop over a skittle, knocking down a pyramid of tin cans - all the usual things.

6.	You may devise a Challenge that is so exciting and, well, challenging, that people will pay for the privilege of taking part! This might be a marathon session such as a Singathon, or an attempt on a record such as fitting as many people as possible on top of a pillarbox. Whatever it is they should want to be part of it so much that they are prepared to pay an entrance fee. If they are sponsored as well, so much the better!

7.	If you have a particular fund raising drive on, you might challenge each person to raise as much as they can. The target can be divided between the number of members so each person has a minimum achievement to aim for, but each tries for the maximum, of course. You may care to make some arrangement to avoid difficulties if some members have far more, or far fewer, opportunities to raise funds because of their circumstances. It would be most unfortunate if this were to lead to embarrassment for some.

8.	An interesting development of this idea is to adopt the principle of the parable of the talents from the Bible. Each member is given a small sum of money, and challenged to use this to produce as much extra money as possible. Depending on the sum it might be used to buy seeds to grow flowers to sell, or the ingredients for a cake to raffle, or whatever. Members use their imagination, talents, and the seedcorn money to produce a good profit for the organisation.

9.	We have suggested that people might pay to take

part in a challenge, or to benefit from a challenge (by having their car cleaned, for example). Don't forget that Challenges are often great spectator sports. Make the spectators pay!

10. In certain circumstances it may be appropriate to emphasise the importance of succeeding in a Challenge by asking the participant to agree to pay a cash forfeit if he or she fails! This is perhaps most appropriate for adults, and can be used in such circumstances as a challenge to give up smoking or swearing, or to lose weight!

THE PRINTFORCE CHALLENGE

And now, we challenge you! Complete the following problems, and send us your answers on the form at the back of the book. Only entries on these actual forms removed from the book will be valid. There is no closing date.

The first correct entry we receive will gain its sender £100. The senders of the next 5 correct entries received will be sent 10 Printforce books of their choice. All other senders of correct entries will be sent Printforce Discount Vouchers, entitling them to a 30% discount on one copy of each of any books in the Printforce range.

It isn't easy, but it is possible. We challenge you to complete it!

1. "Out of the strong came forth sweetness". From what did the hymenopterous insects emerge?

2. 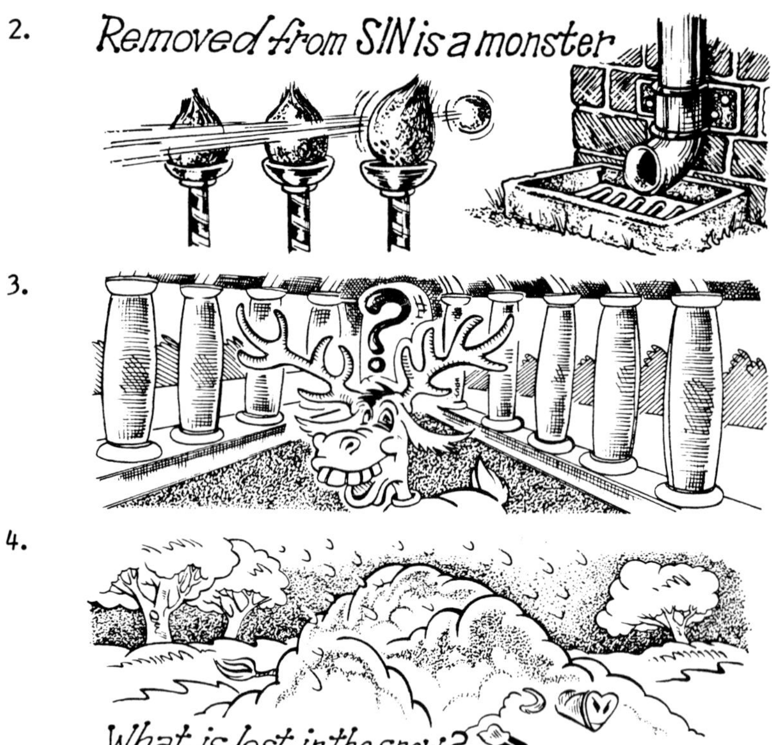

5. P19 L16 W4 + 5

6. What 1963 horror movie could hardly be described as a flight of fancy?

7. *Spit and polish a minotaur*

8. YZ/VU YZ IJ RQ/WX OP/KL XW RQ PO QR PO
    (A=YZ)

9. I hype plot about a queen whose girdle was the
    death of her.

10. 5.5 (EW) 36 (NS)

11. NE2, SE2, NW1, W1/N2, E1, S1, W1/N2, E1, S1,
    W1/S2, E1/W1, N1, E1, W1, N1, E1/E1, N1, W1,
    N1, E1.

12. He dogged the Underworld.

13. To what classic feat is the Printforce Challenge
    somewhat akin?

ANSWER FORM

1. _ _ _ _

2. _ _ _ _ _

3. _ _ _ _ _ _ _   _ _ _ _

4. _ _ _ _

5. _ _ _ _ _ _   _ _ _ _ _ _

6. _ _ _ _ _

7. _ _ _ _

8. _ _ _ _ _ _ _   _ _   _ _ _ _ _ _

9. _ _ _ _ _ _ _ _

10. _ _ _ _ _ _ _   _ _   _ _ _ _ _ _ _ _

11. _ _ _ _ _ _

12. _ _ _ _ _ _ _ _

13. _ _ _   _ _ _ _ _ _ _   _ _ _ _ _ _ _ _   _ _

_ _ _ _ _ _ _ _

Name
Address
Organisation

Age range (please delete as appropriate). Up to 16; 16-20; 20-30; 30-40; 40-50; 50-60; 60+. We would be very pleased if, whilst writing to us, you indicated any additional subjects about which you would like to see a Printforce Book. Thank you.